INTRODUCTION

HMS *Belfast* is a cruiser. She was launched in 1938 and served with distinction in both the Second World War and the Korean War. She is now the only surviving example of the great fleets of big gun armoured warships built for the Royal Navy in the first half of the twentieth century and the first ship to be preserved for the nation since Nelson's flagship, HMS *Victory*.

When delivered in August 1939, *Belfast* represented the high-water mark of British cruiser development and her retirement from active service in 1965 brought down the final curtain on a long line of vessels built to protect the Empire's trade routes during the period of Britain's maritime ascendency.

As you tour this great warship you will probably be amazed by her sheer size and the complexity of the machinery and equipment which made HMS *Belfast* one of the most powerful vessels of her type afloat. But please spare a thought for her

Robert Crawford, Director General of the Imperial War Museum (right) and Jon Wenzel, Director of HMS *Belfast*. IWM Neg. No. 96/75/1

crew. At the height of her operational service at the end of the Second World War, HMS *Belfast* was home to over 950 officers and men. Apart from the threat posed by enemy action, whether from German surface warships, U-Boats, aircraft, mines or torpedoes, HMS *Belfast*'s

crew also had to confront the ever-present menace of that most remorseless and pitiless of all enemies – the sea. Packed into her unyielding, yet all too vulnerable steel hull, her crew endured the most uncomfortable and, at times, squalid conditions as HMS *Belfast* cruised the oceans of the world in the twilight of Britain's Imperial epoch.

In all her many and varied aspects, HMS *Belfast* is a vital and enduring reminder of the reality of naval warfare in the twentieth century. As Director, it is my pleasure to welcome you on board in the certain knowledge that your support will help to ensure that future generations will be able to experience the wonder of this great, historic warship.

Jon Wenzel
Director
HMS *Belfast*

YOUR VISIT TO

WELCOME ON BOARD HMS *BELFAST*!

The purpose of this chapter is to help you to find your way around this huge and complex warship and to get the most out of your tour. Even though at least half of the vessel cannot be opened to the public for reasons of safety, there are still seven decks to explore and it is all too easy for visitors to get confused and to miss out on seeing key areas of the ship.

Below **The Director and members of HMS *Belfast*'s staff beneath the ship's forward 6-inch Gun Turrets.** IWM Neg. No. 95/10/7

Right **Ship's cat. When first commissioned, HMS *Belfast* was authorised to carry three ship's cats. Visitors can see two of these in model form, but you may be lucky enough to encounter the real ship's cat, whose job it is to discourage the ingress of mice and rats from the shore.
HMS *Belfast*'s cats are always carefully chosen for their friendly and affectionate natures but visitors with small children should remember that they are working animals and may not take kindly to rough or insensitive handling.**

REDEVELOPMENT First of all, an apology. HMS *Belfast* is currently undergoing a comprehensive programme of redevelopment which will not be complete until the year 2000. Every effort will be made to keep this guide and all other sources of information about the ship as up to date as possible but we apologise for any inaccuracies or closures to exhibitions and displays which you may encounter on your visit.

THE VISITORS' ROUTE To help you find your way around HMS *Belfast*, the ship has been divided into eight zones. These are detailed opposite and in the ticket/guide leaflet which is made available to all visitors. Though you are free to plan your own route through the ship, it is suggested that you visit each zone in sequence, starting from the ship's Quarterdeck (Zone 1). Each zone is colour coded and you will encounter directional signs at frequent intervals during your tour. In addition, you will find a number of Video Information Monitors, explaining certain technical aspects of HMS *Belfast*'s operation, which also include information about the visitors' route. If you should get lost, please do not hesitate to ask a member of staff for directions.

ZONE 4

ZONE Y Turret

Your tour will take you from HMS *Belfast*'s Quarterdeck up to the top of her Bridge and all the way down to her massive Boiler and Engine Rooms, located well below the ship's waterline. On your way, you will be able to see inside her triple 6–inch Gun Turrets; operate her light anti-aircraft guns; explore the heavily armoured Shell Rooms and Magazines; and experience what life was like for her crew by visiting the cramped Messdecks, Officers' Cabins, Galley and Sick Bay.

We hope that you will enjoy your visit to HMS *Belfast*. Children must be supervised at all times when exploring the interior of the ship. Please be careful and do mind your head when using the ship's ladders.

HMS *BELFAST*

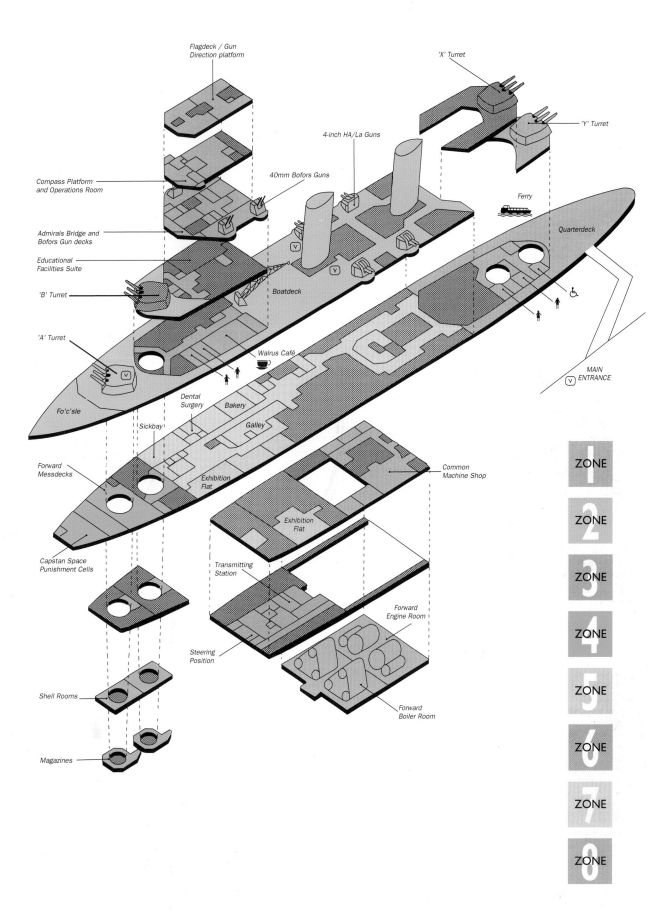

Flagdeck / Gun Direction platform

'X' Turret

'Y' Turret

4-inch HA/La Guns

40mm Bofors Guns

Compass Platform and Operations Room

Ferry

Quarterdeck

Admirals Bridge and Bofors Gun decks

Educational Facilities Suite

'B' Turret

Boatdeck

'A' Turret

MAIN ENTRANCE

Fo'c'sle

Walrus Café

Dental Surgery

Bakery

Sickbay

Galley

Forward Messdecks

Exhibition Flat

Common Machine Shop

Exhibition Flat

Capstan Space Punishment Cells

Transmitting Station

Forward Engine Room

Steering Position

Shell Rooms

Forward Boiler Room

Magazines

ZONE 1

ZONE 2

ZONE 3

ZONE 4

ZONE 5

ZONE 6

ZONE 7

ZONE 8

TOUR OF

ZONE

THE QUARTERDECK

Your tour of HMS *Belfast* begins here. Officers and ratings always salute when stepping onto the Quarterdeck of a Royal Naval vessel. It was here that flag officers, captains of ships and others who were entitled to the honour were 'piped' on board and where guards and bands were paraded. The Quarterdeck on HMS *Belfast* was 'Officer Country' and ratings were not normally permitted to set foot on it except when on duty or to attend the regular Sunday church services presided over by the Captain of the ship. This tradition of worship is maintained when

Below **The ship's honours board.**

Bottom **The silver ship's bell was presented by the citizens of Belfast in 1948.**

Top right **Officers and men gathered on the Quarterdeck of a British cruiser for a church service held at sea during the Second World War.**
IWM Neg. No. A 11316

Bottom right **The interior of 'Y' Turret, showing the shells and cordite charges ready to be rammed into the open breeches of the 6-inch guns.**

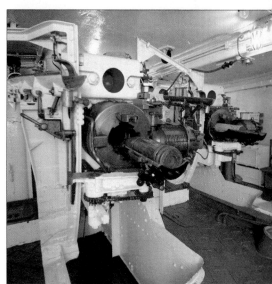

each November the Quarterdeck is the setting for HMS *Belfast*'s annual Remembrance Day Service.

The White Ensign is flown here day and night by all Royal Naval vessels at sea, and from 'Colours' (8.00 am in summer, 9.00 am in winter) to sunset when in harbour.

SHIP'S BATTLE HONOURS AND SILVER BELL

Next to the Quartermaster's Lobby, you will see the board which lists HMS *Belfast*'s battle honours beneath her crest and the motto *Pro Tanto Quid Retribuamus* (What shall we give in return for so much?), which is also the motto of the city of Belfast where the ship was built.

The ship's silver bell was presented by the people of Belfast in October 1948. On the

inner rim of the bell are the names of those children born to serving officers and sailors and christened on board, when the upturned bell was used as a font. When HMS *Belfast* was in service the original ship's bell, which is not on view, was sounded every half-hour to mark the passing of each watch.

'Y' TURRET

Overlooking the Quarterdeck are 'X' and 'Y' Turrets, the after pair of HMS *Belfast*'s four 6-inch Mark XXIII Triple Gun Turrets. 'Y' Turret is open to visitors.

GUNNERY OFFICE

In the cabin flat below the after turrets, you can see a young officer dressing for dinner in the Gunnery Office. Public toilets, including facilities for the disabled, are located nearby.

THE SHIP

ZONE 2

Access to Zone 2 can be gained from either side of the Quarter-deck. A ramp for disabled visitors is provided on the starboard side of the ship.

4-INCH GUNS

HMS *Belfast*'s secondary battery of four Twin 4-inch HA/LA Mark XIX Mountings is located in pairs on either side of the ship between her funnels. During the Second World War, HMS *Belfast* carried six of these mountings but the aftermost pair was removed at the end of the war to make way for additional deckhouses. Although they were primarily designed to protect the ship from attack by enemy aircraft, the guns could also be used against surface targets, hence the designation HA/LA – High Angle/Low Angle. Two Video Information Monitors on either side of the ship provide further details of the operation of the 4-inch HA/LA mountings.

BOATDECK AND MAINMAST

Directly in front of the forward pair of 4-inch mountings lies the great open expanse of HMS *Belfast*'s Boatdeck. When in commission, HMS *Belfast* carried a large number of ship's boats which were hoisted in and out of the water by the 7–ton electric boat crane mounted just aft of the Bridge.

In the early stages of the Second World War, however, the Boatdeck was used as a platform for reconnaissance seaplanes which could be launched by catapult to search for vessels beyond the horizon. After completing a mission, the planes would land in the sea alongside the ship and be lifted back on board by crane. HMS *Belfast* normally carried two seaplanes, each of which was provided with a weather-proof hangar in the wings of the Bridge. Once the ship had been fitted with the long-range search radar which you can see at the top of her Mainmast, there was no further need to carry aircraft on board and in mid-1943 the seaplanes were removed. You can find out more about the operation of HMS *Belfast*'s aircraft by watching either of the Video Information Monitors located next to the 4-inch HA/LA mountings.

On leaving the Boatdeck, you should proceed along the port side of the Bridge towards the bow of the ship and HMS *Belfast*'s Forecastle and forward 6-inch Turrets.

FO'C'SLE AND ANCHORS

The Forecastle, or Fo'c'sle, was originally a raised platform on wooden warships where fighting men would gather to rain down fire upon the decks of enemy ships below. In more recent times the Fo'c'sle has been used primarily for the operation of ships' anchors. HMS *Belfast* once carried three

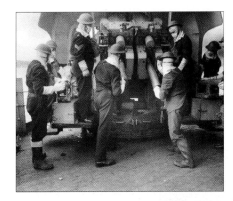

Left **The fixed ammunition shells for HMS *Belfast*'s 4-inch HA/LA mountings weighed 66 pounds (30 kg) and were loaded manually into the breeches of the guns. The shells had to be punched home with a clenched fist as the breech blocks closed automatically and could easily crush the fingers of an open hand. A well-trained gun crew was expected to be able to maintain an average rate of fire of 10 rounds per minute per gun.** IWM Neg. No. A 16317

Below **HMS *Belfast*'s Seaplane Flight, 700 Squadron Fleet Air Arm, pictured in front of one of the ship's Supermarine Walrus Mark I amphibians.** IWM Neg. No. HU 447700

anchors, two on the starboard bow and one on the port. One of the starboard anchors (the sheet anchor) was removed in 1940 and now only the port anchor (weighing 5.5 tons) can be seen stowed on the deck. The anchor cables pass around the cable-holders before disappearing into the Cable Locker below, where they can be seen later on in your tour in Zone 4.

HMS *Belfast*'s anchors were usually raised and lowered by electric power but in an emergency large wooden bars could be inserted into the capstan to operate the machinery manually. It took the combined efforts of 144 men to raise the ship's anchors by this method. Today HMS *Belfast* is permanently moored to the river bed but she still rises and falls about 20 feet (6–7 metres) every day as the tides ebb and flood.

In common with all Royal Naval vessels in harbour, HMS *Belfast* flies the Union Flag daily between 'Colours' and sunset from the jack-staff at her bow.

'A' TURRET

Overlooking the Fo'c'sle, you will see 'A' and 'B' Turrets, the forwardmost of HMS *Belfast*'s four 6-inch Mark XXIII Triple Gun Turrets. 'A' Turret is open to visitors and there is a Video Information Monitor inside which will tell you all about the complex operation of the ship's main armament. The guns in both Turrets are trained and elevated onto a target some 12.5 miles (20 kilometers) away in north-west London – the Scratchwood Motorway Services Area on the M1 – a reminder of the awsome power of naval gunnery in the Second World War.

You should now return along the starboard side of the ship to the rear of the Bridge, where you will find a ladder which provides access to Zone 3.

 ZONE 3 Between 1956 and 1959, HMS *Belfast* underwent an extended refit and modernization which resulted in significant alterations to her Bridge superstructure. The original open Bridge was replaced by an enclosed Compass Platform, with a large Operations Room adjacent to it; improved accommodation and command facilities were provided for the Admiral and his staff, and modern close-range anti-aircraft guns were mounted on top of the Bridge wings which had once served as hangars for HMS *Belfast*'s seaplanes. Nevertheless, the essential functions of the Bridge remained largely unchanged, with only the introduction of more sophisticated electronic equipment to mark the passage of time between the last years of HMS *Belfast*'s active life and her days of front-line service in the Second World War.

40MM BOFORS GUNS AND CLOSE RANGE BLIND FIRE DIRECTORS

On either side of the Bridge wings are two 40 mm Twin Bofors Mark V Mountings. In all, HMS *Belfast* was equipped with six of these mountings during the course of her modernization, the two additional mounts being located on her after superstructure. Three of the four Bofors mountings can be trained and elevated by hand, although very young children may need some assistance as each mounting weighs almost 7 tons! Fire from the guns was controlled by two Close Range Blind Fire Directors (CRBFDs), which are best seen from the top of the Bridge.

BRIDGE WIRELESS OFFICE

On the same level as the Bridge wings, you can see the Bridge Wireless Office (BWO), where all incoming radio messages were received and outgoing messages transmitted. The BWO is still used today by the Royal Naval Amateur Radio Society and enthusiasts

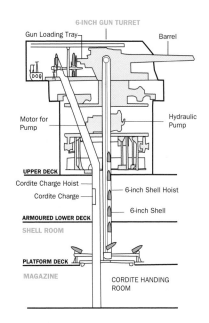

Diagram labels:
6-INCH GUN TURRET
Gun Loading Tray
Barrel
Motor for Pump
Hydraulic Pump
UPPER DECK
Cordite Charge Hoist
Cordite Charge
6-inch Shell Hoist
6-inch Shell
ARMOURED LOWER DECK
SHELL ROOM
PLATFORM DECK
MAGAZINE
CORDITE HANDING ROOM

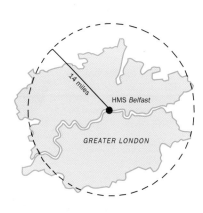

14 miles

HMS *Belfast*

GREATER LONDON

Top **Cross-section of a 6-inch Mark XXIII Triple Mounting, illustrating ammunition supply.**

Above **The range of the ship's 6-inch guns.**

Top Right **Visitors elevating and training one of the 40 mm Bofors guns.** IWM Neg. No. MH 34013

Right **The Flag Deck was controlled by the Yeoman of Signals, who would pass messages to other vessels in sight using flags, semaphore or Morse code on a signal projector. In this picture, taken on board HMS *Sheffield* in 1941, ice is forming on the projector making the signalman's task extremely difficult.** IWM Neg. No. A 6872

can contact them in HMS *Belfast* by using the ship's international call sign, GB2RN. The Electronic Warfare Office, which housed equipment designed to confuse enemy radar and radio signals, is located next to the BWO.

Please mind your head when using the ladders outside the BWO to continue your ascent to the top of the Bridge. Here you will find the Flag Deck, Gunnery Direction Platform and, overlooking them, the Fore-mast and Forward Director Control Tower.

FLAG DECK AND FOREMAST

The Flag Deck was used to send visual signals to nearby vessels. The 10-inch and 20-inch signalling projectors on either side of the deck flashed messages in Morse code and the Foremast was used to hoist communications by flags. HMS *Belfast* was original-ly equipped with lightweight tripod masts but these were replaced by much stronger lattice masts in order to support the weight of the radar systems fitted to the ship after modernization.

FORWARD DIRECTOR CONTROL TOWER

The Forward Director Control Tower (DCT) controlled the operation of all four of HMS *Belfast*'s 6-inch Gun Turrets. Originally, the DCT was fitted with a large optical range-finder, but from 1942 onwards targets were normally acquired and tracked by radar.

A second DCT, mounted on the after superstructure, was provided to control the independent operation of the two after Turrets.

GUN DIRECTION PLATFORM

In good visibility, all of HMS *Belfast*'s guns could be controlled from the Gun Direction Platform (GDP) at the forward end of the upper bridge. The Captain's sight on the centre platform was used to indicate targets to the Director Control Tower and the GDP offered an unrivalled vantage point for look-outs manning the four circular sights to search the sea and sky with their binoculars.

You should now begin your descent to the lower levels of the Bridge using the lad-der immediately in front of the Director Control Tower. Please mind your head.

OPERATIONS ROOM AND COMPASS PLATFORM

On the deck below are HMS *Belfast*'s Oper-ations Room and Compass Platform, the nerve centre and brain of the entire ship. Although the layout and equipment in both these areas differs from that fitted in the Second World War, the plots and 'state-boards' have been reconstructed to show HMS *Belfast*'s role in the Battle of North Cape on 26 December 1943, which ended in the sinking of the German battle-cruiser *Scharnhorst*. You can also hear a sound effect which reconstructs key moments dur-ing the course of the battle, wherever possi-ble using original Admiralty signals and drawing upon the recollections of members of HMS *Belfast*'s crew who took part in the engagement.

Above **The entire operation of the ship could be controlled from the Compass Platform by the Officer of the Watch. The Captain would usually take command when the ship was in action or carrying out dangerous manoeuvres.**

Left **View from the open bridge of HMS *Sheffield*, one of HMS *Belfast*'s half-sisters, as she fights her way through heavy seas on convoy duty in the North Atlantic in 1943.** IWM Neg. No. A 14890

Below **The Operations Room as it might have appeared during the Battle of North Cape. The sailors are wearing anti-flash hoods and gloves to protect their faces and hands from the severe burns which could be caused by an enemy shell exploding on the Bridge.**

Above **Rear-Admiral (later Admiral) Sir Robert Burnett, who flew his flag in HMS *Belfast* at the time of the Battle of North Cape.** IWM Neg. No. A 12758

Right **The Captain's sea cabin. The figure of the Captain is modelled on Captain (later Admiral Sir Frederick) Parham, who commanded HMS *Belfast* from November 1942 to July 1944.**

Below **A typical sea cabin. The officer handing a mug of scalding hot naval cocoa (known as 'Ki') to his colleague is a Captain of the Royal Marines. The red lighting – 'darken ship routine' – is intended to preserve the crew's night vision when in action and to ensure that HMS *Belfast* shows no bright lights which might betray her position to the enemy.**

In the Operations Room, information derived from radar, sonar and intelligence reports on Allied and enemy surface, submarine and air forces was collated and displayed on plots and 'stateboards'. From this combined information, the Captain was able to evaluate the tactical situation and respond accordingly.

It was from the Compass Platform that the Captain or Officer of the Watch controlled the ship at sea, passing steering and engine orders to the helmsman at the wheel in the Forward Steering Position, located six decks below in Zone 6. The ship's course was plotted by the Navigating Officer and his assistants in the Charthouse at the back of the Compass Platform.

ADMIRAL'S BRIDGE AND OFFICERS' SEA CABINS

On the deck below the Compass Platform are the Admiral's Bridge and the sea cabins reserved for the Admiral and his staff and for the Captain. HMS *Belfast* was built as a flagship and carried an Admiral for most of

her operational life. The additional bridge was provided so that the Admiral and his staff could exercise control over the fleet or squadron of vessels under his command without overcrowding the Compass Platform and interfering with the operation of the ship.

As well as their main cabins, located beneath HMS *Belfast*'s Quarterdeck, the Admiral and the Captain were also provided with sea cabins where they could work and sleep when the ship was in action or taking part in exercises. There are additional sea cabins for less senior officers on the deck below.

You should now descend to the lowest level of the Bridge, where you will find the ship's cafeteria, the Walrus Café, as well as Ladies and Gents toilets. Access to Zone 4 is via a ladder leading down from the forward end of the Bridge superstructure.

 ZONE 4 You are now standing on HMS *Belfast*'s Upper (No. 2) Deck, the ship's main accommodation deck. Please proceed towards the bow of the ship and the Forward Messdecks.

6-INCH BARBETTES

As you walk towards the bow, you will be able to see the huge armoured cylinders, known as barbettes, which protected the 6-inch ammunition hoists bringing shells and cordite charges up to 'A' and 'B' Turrets from the Shell Rooms and Magazines below. The sides of the barbettes are composed of 2-inch (51 mm) plates of armour.

Access to the Shell Rooms is via a ladder just aft of 'A' Turret barbette, but it is suggested that you delay your visit until after you have seen all of the messdecks.

FORWARD MESSDECKS

When HMS *Belfast* was first commissioned, a sailor's life was in many respects little changed from the days of Nelson. Sailors joined the Navy at 16 and signed initially for a 12-year engagement, starting from the age of 18. Pay for an Able Seaman was just 21 shillings (£1.05) per week, out of which married men were required to make an allowance of 3 shillings and sixpence (17p) to their wives. A sailor received an additional 12 shillings and sixpence (62p) for each child, and a marriage allowance of 18 shillings (90p) per week was paid direct to his wife while he was at sea. Even allowing for the lower cost of living, the wages of an Able Seaman were barely sufficient to keep his family above the poverty line.

Like their predecessors in Nelson's time, HMS *Belfast*'s ratings lived, slept and ate in communal areas known as messes, which were crammed into every available space. While officers were allocated cabins, the ratings slung their hammocks in their mess or slept where they could around the ship. Despite the fact that hammocks were slung only 21 inches (52 cm) apart, the hugely enlarged crews required in wartime (HMS *Belfast*'s authorised peacetime complement of 761 had increased to over 950 by the end of the Second World War) meant that it was not at all unusual for men on different watches to share the use of a hammock or to sleep on the deck beneath one of the mess tables.

Until the 1950s, large warships such as HMS *Belfast* operated a catering system known as Broadside Messing. Each mess would appoint a duty cook who would collect the basic meal for his messmates from the galley, return to his mess, serve it and wash up before returning the empty containers to the galley. Each mess had an allowance to purchase additional or 'luxury' items of food and the ship's supply officer – the 'Pusser' – would present an account for payment at the end of each month. Naval food was stodgy and unimaginative but there was generally plenty of it and many messes preferred to save up their allowance for a first-class binge when they had the opportunity to go on shore.

CAPSTAN MACHINERY SPACE AND PUNISHMENT CELLS

The Capstan Machinery Space is situated almost in the bow of the ship and contains the electric motors, gears and vertical shafts which drove the capstans on the Fo'c'sle above (Zone 2). You can see the wooden capstan bars, which were used to turn the capstans by hand in the event of a mechanical breakdown, stowed overhead. Despite this mass of machinery, the compartment was home to 33 sailors, a clear indication of the lack of suitable living space for her crew at the height of HMS *Belfast*'s operational service.

At the forward end of this compartment are the ship's Punishment Cells. The Captain had the power to sentence offenders to periods of up to 14 days' imprisonment for offences such as sleeping on watch, drunkenness or leave-breaking.

On the deck nearby, you can look down through a small access hatch into the Cable Locker where the ship's anchor cables were stowed.

While serving in the North Atlantic during the Second World War, it was not unusual for HMS *Belfast* to encounter hurricane conditions with waves up to 50 feet high. Before leaving the Capstan Machinery Space to visit the Shell Rooms and Magazines, you may like to pause for a moment and imagine what it must have been like to live in this compartment as HMS *Belfast* struggled to lift her bow from beneath the great masses of water foaming over her Fo'c'sle before plunging down to meet the shock of yet another mountainous wave.

Top Left **Breakfast in a seaman's mess on board the battleship HMS *Rodney* during the Second World War.** IWM Neg. No. A 2219

Left **A typical messdeck scene during the Second World War, illustrating the art of climbing into a hammock in a confined space.** IWM Neg. No. A 2216

Below **One of the ship's punishment cells in rough weather.** IWM Neg. No. 96/75/3

Bottom **The Forward Messdecks as they might have appeared when HMS *Belfast* was serving with the Home Fleet in Arctic waters during the Second World War.** IWM Neg. No. 96/75/4

Above **Interior of 'B' Turret Shell Room, showing the 6-inch projectiles lined up on the handling carousel which revolved around the mechanical hoists leading to the gun house above.**

Top right **Rum had been a regular part of the Royal Navy's diet since the capture of Jamaica in 1655. Originally, sailors received no less than half a pint a day of neat spirit, but in 1740 Admiral Edward Vernon introduced the issue of 'grog' (two parts water to one part rum) which remained one of the great traditions of naval life until as late as 1970.**

Below right **'Up spirits!' The rum ration is issued to each mess.**
IWM Neg. No. A 1777

SHELL ROOMS AND MAGAZINES

Please use the ladders leading down from just behind 'A' Turret barbette to enter the Shell Rooms and Magazines, which are located well below the ship's waterline and are the most heavily protected of all the ship's compartments. Apart from the vertical protection against shell-fire provided by the main armour belt, 4.5 inches (114 mm) thick, the deck immediately above the Shell Rooms is also armoured to a thickness of 3 inches (76 mm) to provide protection against aerial bombs.

Each of the 6-inch Gun Turrets is served by its own Shell Room and Magazine, with the Magazines and their vulnerable cordite charges sited below the Shell Rooms on the Hold Deck, the lowest of all HMS *Belfast*'s seven habitable decks. The shells and cordite charges were sent up to the turrets above by mechanical hoists.

Although access to the Magazines and their enclosed Handling Rooms is not permitted for reasons of safety, you can look down into their confined interiors through two hatches, one in each Shell Room. In the event of HMS *Belfast* receiving a hit which threatened an explosion in the Magazines, the compartments could be rapidly flooded to prevent the loss of the ship. In such circumstances, the men working in the

Handling Rooms would have had little chance of escape.

Please use the ladders at the after end of 'B' Turret Shell Room to return to the Upper (No. 2) Deck, where your tour of the ship continues.

PROVISION ISSUE ROOM

As you leave Zone 4 you will pass the Provision Issue Room. For the majority of HMS *Belfast*'s crew this was the most important compartment in the entire ship for it was here that the daily rum ration was measured and prepared for issue in a ritual dating back to the middle of the eighteenth century.

 ZONE 5 Located on the starboard side of the ship, the galleries of the Exhibition Flats on the Upper (No. 2) and Lower (No. 3) Decks illustrate aspects of HMS *Belfast*'s history and the story of the Royal Navy in the twentieth century.

We apologise for the fact that the galleries on the Lower (No. 3) Deck are currently undergoing refurbishment and redevelopment.

HMS *BELFAST* IN WAR AND PEACE

This major exhibition tells the story of the ship from her inception in the late 1930s to the decision to save her for the nation in 1971. Using original artefacts, documents, plans and drawings as well as contemporary paintings and photographs, ship models and audio-visual displays, *HMS Belfast in War and Peace* provides a comprehensive account of this great historic warship and of the men who served in her.

THE ROYAL NAVY TODAY

An exhibition mounted by the Navy Department of the ministry of Defence which illustrates the role and equipment of today's navy and compares the fighting power of HMS *Belfast* with that of a modern guided missile frigate, HMS *Chatham*.

ZONE 6 The direction signs will take you down to the Platform (No. 4) Deck amidships. This area, located well below the water-line and protected by two inches (51 mm) of horizontal armour, houses some of the most important compartments in the ship.

6-INCH TRANSMITTING STATION

The Transmitting Station (TS) was a vital component in the complex system which controlled the operation of HMS *Belfast*'s main armament. In the middle of the compartment, surrounded by its associated radar displays, is the Admiralty Fire Control Table (AFCT), a mechanical computer designed in the 1930s. Information provided by the Forward Director Control Tower on the Bridge (Zone 3) about the range and bearing of an enemy ship was fed into the AFCT, which then calculated the correct angles of train and elevation required for the guns in all four turrets to hit their target.

A smaller version of the AFCT, known as the Admiralty Fire Control Clock (AFCC), is located next door and provided similar data for the after turrets only.

FORWARD CONVERSION MACHINERY ROOM

HMS *Belfast* used both direct (DC) and alternating (AC) electric current to power her equipment. The AC current, which supplied her gyro compass, gunnery control systems, radar and wireless equipment, was converted in this compartment and distributed from the switchboard on the other side of the 6-inch Transmitting Station.

FORWARD GYRO COMPASS ROOM

The navigation compass in this compartment worked on the gyroscopic principle which ensured that, whichever way the ship turned, the compass always pointed towards true north. This allowed the ship to be steered accurately and also provided the directional basis for aligning the radars and the gunnery control systems.

Beneath the nearby Soap and Tobacco Store a German magnetic mine exploded on 21 November 1939, almost causing the loss of the ship.

FORWARD STEERING POSITION

HMS *Belfast* was steered from this heavily protected compartment by the ship's helmsman, who received his instructions from the Officer of the Watch on the Compass Platform (Zone 3). The steering motors and the massive hydraulic rams which operated the ship's rudder are located beneath the Quarter-deck in the Tiller Flat.

The ship's telephone exchange can be seen at the back of the compartment.

Please use the ladders outside the Forward Steering Position to return to HMS *Belfast*'s Upper (No. 2) Deck and Zone 7.

Above **German magnetic mine of the type which severely damaged the ship in November 1939 on display in the exhibition *HMS Belfast in War and Peace.***
IWM Neg. No. 96/75/7

Left **This very rare photograph of Royal Marines manning a Transmitting Station in action was taken on board the aircraft carrier HMS *Victorious* during the Second World War.**
IWM Neg. No. A 7640

Below **HMS *Belfast*'s Forward Steering Position. A secondary emergency steering position was located near the Tiller Flat at the stern of the ship.**

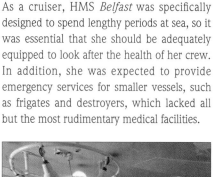

During the course of her extended refit and modernization in the late 1950s, substantial changes were made to the layout of HMS *Belfast*'s Upper (No. 2) Deck amidships, in an attempt to improve the living conditions of her crew in the post-war era. In Zone 7 you can see how HMS *Belfast* looked near the end of her active life, when she was serving mainly in the Far East.

SICKBAY AND DENTAL SURGERY

As a cruiser, HMS *Belfast* was specifically designed to spend lengthy periods at sea, so it was essential that she should be adequately equipped to look after the health of her crew. In addition, she was expected to provide emergency services for smaller vessels, such as frigates and destroyers, which lacked all but the most rudimentary medical facilities.

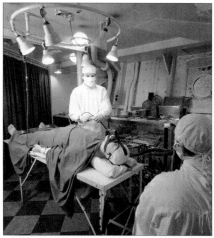

Above **The NAAFI Canteen sold a wide variety of goods. It was usually busy one day in each fortnight – pay day!**

Top right **The Surgeon Commander carries out an emergency operation in the ship's operating theatre.**

Right **The Dental Officer was usually a Surgeon Lieutenant Commander and was an important member of the ship's general medical team, but his main task was to look after the dental health of the ship's company.**

NAAFI CANTEEN

Since 1921, the Navy Army and Air Force Institute's (NAAFI) Naval Canteen Service has served the Royal Navy both ashore and afloat. Large warships such as HMS *Belfast* were equipped with well-stocked canteens selling a wide variety of goods, including duty-free tobacco, confectionery and small luxury items, as well as essentials such as toothpaste and shoe polish. Wine and spirits were not permitted, but, from 1960 onwards, each member of the crew could purchase up to two cans of beer a day, provided the cans were opened immediately to prevent hoarding. A percentage of the profits generated from this enterprise went towards a general ship's fund, known as the canteen fund, administered by a committee for the benefit of the whole crew.

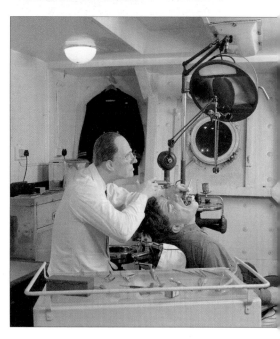

Following modernization, HMS *Belfast* was authorised to carry a medical complement of two officers and up to five sick-berth attendants, including a radiographer and physiotherapist. The operating theatre was sufficiently well equipped, with its own small X-ray machine, for the Surgeon Commander to perform most routine operations but it was normally only used in emergencies because of the movement and vibration of the ship. No such inhibitions seem to have affected the work of his deputy, the Dental Officer!

during her service as flagship in the Far East was extremely limited, and she was constantly expected to act as 'mother' to her smaller charges, providing them with essential foodstuffs from her capacious stores. So each day a staff of six bakers had the mammoth task of producing sufficient bread, not only for HMS *Belfast*'s crew, but also for the crews of smaller vessels which had no means of baking bread.

In the darkened Potato Store next door, you can see one of the ship's cats at work!

SHIP'S COMPANY GALLEY

The Ship's Company Galley dates from the period after HMS *Belfast*'s modernization, when meals for the crew were prepared by properly trained and qualified staff and served from the counter – a practice known as General or Cafeteria Messing. This system resulted in a dramatic improvement in the quality and variety of meals served in HM warships and reflected the much better living conditions which were expected by sailors in the post-war navy.

Instead of taking their meals in their mess, the crew now ate in a common canteen – the Ship's Company Dining Hall. The galley staff were supplemented by ratings from each department of the ship, who were detailed to work in the Vegetable Preparation Room.

Additional galleys serving the officers in the Wardroom and the Admiral's Dining Room were located further aft.

BAKERY, POTATO STORE AND BEEF SCREEN

On the starboard side of the ship, immediately opposite the Ship's Company Galley, are a number of compartments devoted to the provisioning of HMS *Belfast* in her last years of active service.

Stowage space in many of the ships which sailed in company with HMS *Belfast*

The Beef Screen served as the ship's butcher's shop. HMS *Belfast* was authorised to carry two trained Royal Marine butchers, who also kept an eye on the refrigerated Galley Ready Use Store.

ENTRANCE TO ZONE 8

Although Zone 7 continues all the way through to the ship's Quarterdeck and main exit, you may wish to make a detour at this point in order to visit HMS *Belfast*'s Forward Boiler and Engine Rooms. Access to Zone 8 is via a hatchway next to the small Lending Library, at the after end of the Ship's Company Galley.

Top right **A 21-inch Mark IX torpedo being fired from one of the ship's triple torpedo mountings during sea trials in 1939.** IWM Neg. No. HU 16022

Right **While church services for the entire ship's company were generally held on the Quarterdeck, this small Chapel was available for private prayer and could be used by men of all religious faiths.**

Below **The ship's Mail Room.**

Bottom **One of HMS *Belfast*'s volunteer Chinese stewards at work in the ship's Laundry.** IWM Neg. No. 96/75/2

SRE, CHAPEL AND MAILROOM

HMS *Belfast*'s Sound Reproduction Equipment Room (SRE) was used at the end of her active life to entertain her crew with popular music and radio programmes.

By tradition, all large Royal Navy warships have an area set aside as a chapel. The ship's Chaplain was an important member of the crew, acting as a friend and adviser to sailors of all religious denominations. HMS *Belfast*'s Chapel is still occasionally used for christenings and for private worship.

Next door to the Chapel you can see the ship's Mail Room.

SHIP'S LAUNDRY AND 21-INCH TORPEDO

Throughout most of her active life, HMS *Belfast*'s crew were expected to wash their own clothes in buckets and basins, and it was not until her extended refit and modernization in the late 1950s that a well-equipped laundry was finally installed. When the ship was in the Far East, locally recruited Chinese were often employed as laundrymen and, by tragic irony, one of these unfortunate volunteers was killed and four wounded when HMS *Belfast* was struck by shells from a Communist shore battery during the Korean War.

On the starboard side of the ship, next to the Laundry, you can see an example of a 21-inch Mark IX Torpedo. HMS *Belfast* originally carried six of these weapons in

two triple revolving mounts, sited between her funnels, just a bit further forward from where you are now standing. The torpedo mountings were removed and their firing ports plated over during her 1950s' refit.

ZONE 8 HMS *Belfast*'s main propulsive machinery is laid out according to a system first introduced by the United States Navy, known as Unit Propulsion. This system was based upon the grouping together of the boilers and engines into self-contained units – in HMS *Belfast*'s case, four boilers and four engines arranged in pairs (Boiler Room/ Engine Room, Boiler Room/Engine Room), in four separate but cross-connected watertight compartments – so that a single hit from an enemy shell or torpedo could never disable more than 50% of the ship's power plant. HMS *Belfast*'s after pair of Boiler and Engine Rooms is closed for reasons of safety but the Forward Boiler and Engine Rooms have been restored and are permanently open to visitors. Access is via a massive hatchway in the main armoured deck, 2 inches (51 mm) thick, at the after end of the Ship's Company Galley.

FORWARD BOILER ROOM

The entrance to the Forward Boiler Room is guarded by a double set of doors forming an airlock into the huge compartment beyond. This was essential as any sudden change in air pressure could result in the boilers 'flashing back' and incinerating anything, or anyone, in front of them. Once through these doors, you can descend through a maze of pipework and trunking to the floor of the Boiler Room, three decks below. Please be careful when negotiating the ladders in this compartment.

HMS *Belfast*'s boilers burned a heavy oil mixture, known as Furnace Fuel Oil (FFO), to produce super-heated steam at a pressure of 350 pounds per square inch. The steam was then piped through to the

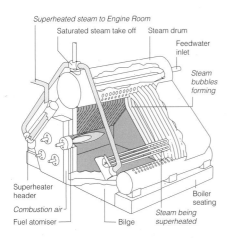

Superheated steam to Engine Room
Saturated steam take off — Steam drum
Feedwater inlet
Steam bubbles forming
Superheater header
Combustion air
Fuel atomiser — Bilge
Boiler seating
Steam being superheated

A boiler - simplified diagram.

turbine engines, which in turn drove the propeller shafts. It took about four hours to raise sufficient steam to get the ship under way.

Each boiler consisted of three drums; the two lower drums contained water, which was passed through the furnace in steel tubes. The steam generated was collected in the third drum on the top of the boiler. The front cover of one of the water drums on the port side boiler has been removed so that visitors can look inside.

One of HMS *Belfast*'s steam-driven turbo-generators, which provided electric power for the ship when she was at sea, can be seen on the middle level of the Boiler Room, with its turbine and gearbox covers lifted for inspection. Other auxiliary machinery in this compartment includes the fire and bilge pump which drew sea water into the ship's fire mains and pumped out the bilge beneath the machinery.

Please leave the Forward Boiler Room by the ladders leading up on the starboard side of the compartment – **not** the ladders you used to enter – to reach a winding passageway leading to the Forward Engine Room.

SHIP'S COMPANY WASHROOMS

On your way to the Forward Engine Room, you will pass by the washrooms and showers provided for the use of HMS *Belfast*'s crew as well as an emergency exit leading back up to the Upper (No. 2) Deck and Zone 7.

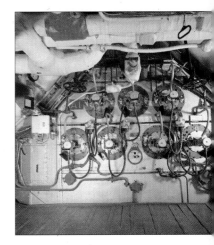

Top left **Simplified diagram of a ship's boiler.**

Above **The oil fuel burners seen here pumped heated Furnace Fuel Oil into the furnace of the boiler in a fine spray. At full speed, HMS *Belfast*'s boilers consumed up to 30 tons of fuel per hour.**

Left **Although the Forward Boiler Room, seen here, was kept surprisingly cool by efficient forced draught ventilation, the noise was deafening and the smell of fuel oil in the bilges could be nauseating to the inexperienced.**

FORWARD ENGINE ROOM

HMS *Belfast* has four propeller shafts, the two outer ones driven by the engines in the Forward Engine Room and the inner ones driven by the engines in the After Engine Room. Each of the four turbine engines is capable of generating 20,000 shaft horsepower, making a total of 80,000 shp (an average family car develops 100 hp), enough to drive HMS *Belfast* through the water at 32 knots – 36 mph (58 kph).

Each engine has four distinct turbine rotors: the two large high and low pressure turbines, which worked in series to develop full power ahead; a small cruising turbine for more economical speeds; and an astern turbine. The super-heated steam from the boilers could be directed to the desired combination of rotors by means of control throttles, driving the turbines, which in turn drove the propeller shafts through the gearbox mechanism attached to each engine.

The auxiliary machinery in this compartment includes a steam-powered turbo-generator and a set of twin evaporators, which were used to distil sea water for the boilers and for domestic purposes.

Please use the ladder at the forward end of the Engine Room, near the control position, to continue your tour.

COMMON MACHINE SHOP

This workshop supplied the needs of all the ship's technical departments and some of the equipment on view is still used today by the ship's maintenance staff.

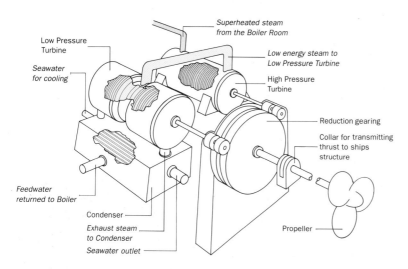

Top **A boiler room in the battleship HMS *Prince of Wales* in 1941.**
IWM Neg. No. A 3912

Above **Simplified diagram of a ship's engine, illustrating the high and low pressure turbines working in series.**

Right **The Engine Officer of the Watch occupied a control position between the two engines in the Forward Engine Room. From here, he could communicate with the Bridge, the After Engine Room and both Boiler Rooms.**

Diagram labels: Low Pressure Turbine; Seawater for cooling; Superheated steam from the Boiler Room; Low energy steam to Low Pressure Turbine; High Pressure Turbine; Reduction gearing; Collar for transmitting thrust to ships structure; Feedwater returned to Boiler; Condenser; Exhaust steam to Condenser; Seawater outlet; Propeller

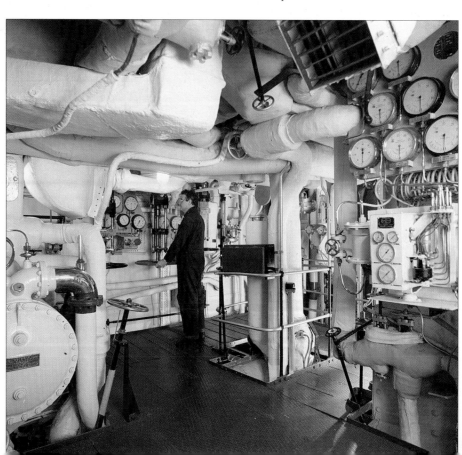

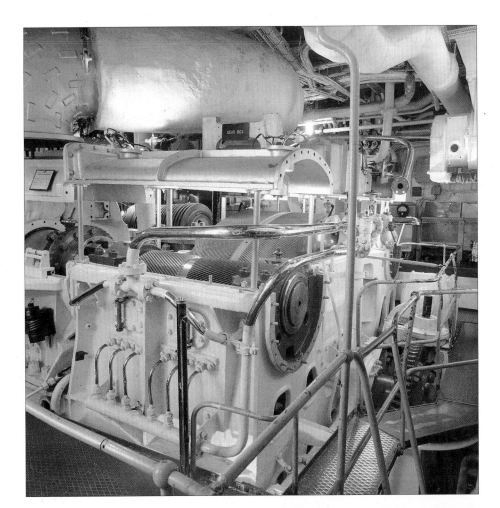

Left The housings have been raised to enable visitors to see the insides of the starboard outer engine's massive turbine rotors and gearbox.

Below Maintenance and repair of the ship's hull and engineering equipment was carried out using the machine tools in the Common Machine Shop. Skilled technicians from all HMS *Belfast*'s departments had access to these tools.

On leaving the Common Machine Shop, you will emerge once again on HMS *Belfast*'s Upper (No. 2) Deck at the after end of Zone 7. The main exit taking you back onto the Quarterdeck is signposted to your left.

You are now at the end of your tour of HMS *Belfast*. Please feel free to retrace your steps if you would like to revisit any part of the ship. We hope that you have thoroughly enjoyed your visit to this historic warship.

SOUVENIR SHOP AND FERRY TO TOWER PIER

You may leave the ship either by crossing the gangway to the south bank of the Thames, where you can visit HMS *Belfast*'s souvenir shop, or by the ferry which runs from the starboard side of the Quarterdeck to Tower Pier on the north bank of the river.

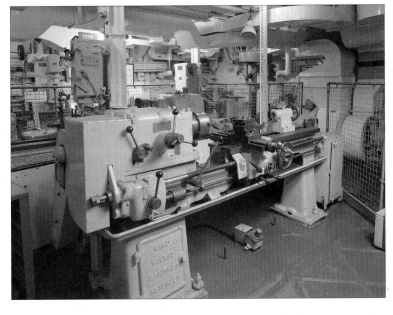

HMS *BELFAST* 1959 – 1965

Illustrated by Ross Watton
© Department of Technical Illustration
Bournemouth & Poole College of Art & Design 1985

SHIP SPECIFICATIONS

CLASS
Edinburgh. Modified Southampton class

SISTER SHIP
HMS *Edinburgh* (sunk May 1942)

BUILT
Harland & Wolff Shipyard, Belfast
Keel laid 10 December 1936

LAUNCHED
17 March 1938 – St. Patrick's Day

COMMISSIONED INTO ROYAL NAVY
5 August 1939

STANDARD DISPLACEMENT
11,553 tons

OVERALL LENGTH
613 feet 6 inches (187 m)

BEAM
69 feet (21 metres)

DRAUGHT
19 feet 9 inches (6.1 metres)

ARMAMENT (1959)
Twelve (4 x 3) 6-inch
Eight (4 x 2) 4-inch HA/LA
Twelve (6 x 2) 40mm Bofors AA

PROPULSIVE MACHINERY
Four Admiralty 3–drum boilers; four
steam powered Parsons single reduction
geared turbines driving four shafts at
80,000 shaft horsepower

MAXIMUM SPEED
32 knots (36 miles/58 km per hour)

COMPLEMENT
750-850 (as flagship)

HISTORY O

ORIGINS OF THE CRUISER

The term 'cruiser' goes back to the days of sailing ships when large frigates could be detached from the main fleet to cruise independently. The sailing cruiser, like her twentieth-century counterpart, was sufficiently powerful and fast to attack and destroy enemy commerce raiders.

During the nineteenth century when sail gave way to steam and wooden ships were replaced by those built of iron, and later of steel, the cruiser evolved into a powerful warship which was used to patrol the Empire trade routes and protect friendly merchant shipping. After the First World War (1914–1918) a single category of cruiser emerged whose size was indicated by the size of its guns; thus, HMS *Belfast* is a 6-inch cruiser, designed for the protection of trade, for offensive action, and as a powerful support for amphibious operations.

HMS *BELFAST,* BUILDING AND LAUNCH

The contract to build HMS *Belfast* was placed on 21 September 1936, and the ship's keel was laid on 10 December 1936, when she became 'Job Number 1000' in Harland & Wolff's shipyard in the city of Belfast. The

Below **'May God bless her and all who sail in her.' With these traditional words Mrs Neville Chamberlain, the wife of the then Prime Minister, launched HMS** *Belfast* **on St Patrick's Day, 17 March 1938 – obviously an auspicious day for a ship built in Northern Ireland. The photograph shows HMS** *Belfast* **just as she enters the water.**
IWM Neg. No. HU 43755

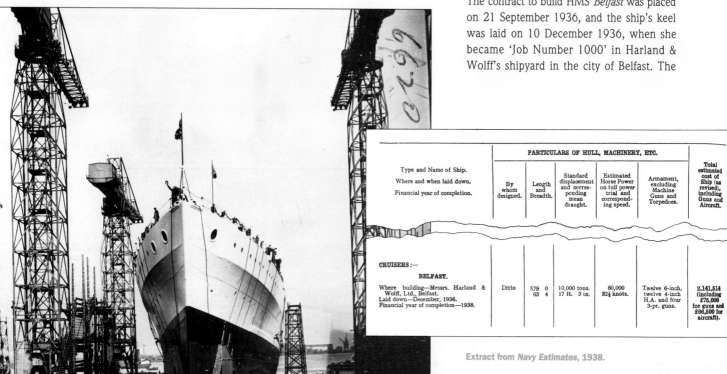

Type and Name of Ship. Where and when laid down. Financial year of completion.	By whom designed.	Length and Breadth.	Standard displacement and corresponding mean draught.	Estimated Horse Power on full power trial and corresponding speed.	Armament, excluding Machine Guns and Torpedoes.	Total estimated cost of Ship (as revised), including Guns and Aircraft.
CRUISERS :—						
BELFAST. Where building—Messrs. Harland & Wolff, Ltd., Belfast. Laid down—December, 1936. Financial year of completion—1938.	Ditto	579 0 63 4	10,000 tons. 17 ft. 3 in.	80,000 32¼ knots.	Twelve 6-inch, twelve 4-inch H.A. and four 3-pr. guns.	2,141,514 (including £75,000 for guns and £66,500 for aircraft).

Extract from *Navy Estimates,* 1938.

Harland and Wolff, Limited.
request the pleasure of the company of
Mr & Mrs J.C. Lee
to witness the Launch of
H.M.S. "Belfast"
on Thursday 17th March 1938, at 11·15 a.m.
from their East Yard
Afterwards to Lunch at 12·30 p.m.
The Naming Ceremony will be performed by
Mrs Neville Chamberlain
Religious Service will commence at 10·55 a.m.
QUEEN'S ISLAND, BELFAST. FEBRUARY 1938. R.S.V.P.

Invitation to the launch of HMS *Belfast,* 1938.

F THE SHIP

navy estimates for 1938 show that her planned cost was £2,141,514, including £75,000 for the guns and £66,500 for aircraft. She was fitted out with all the equipment needed for a modern ship and commissioned on 5 August 1939 under the command of Captain G A Scott DSO RN.

> *'It is upon the Navy, under the Providence of God that the safety, honour and welfare of this realm do chiefly attend.'*
>
> Articles of War, 1666

OUTBREAK OF WAR, 1939

At the outbreak of war with Germany in September 1939, HMS *Belfast* formed part of the 18th Cruiser Squadron based in Scapa Flow in the Orkneys, and the ship was at sea at her war station in the North Atlantic from the very beginning.

In Britain, the first months of the Second World War were often called the 'phoney' war because the opposing armies on the Continent faced each other but without coming to grips. The war at sea was very different. From the start of hostilities, ships of the Royal Navy and Merchant Navy were in action, with frequent contact with enemy ships, aircraft and submarines, and considerable casualties were suffered. On the very first day of the war, the British liner *Athenia* was sunk without warning by the U-boat U30 with heavy loss of life.

As part of her blockade duties on 9 October 1939 HMS *Belfast* intercepted the Norwegian-owned cargo vessel SS *Tai Yin*, which was sent to Kirkwall with an armed guard onboard, and later the same day boarded and captured a German liner, SS *Cap Norte*, which was disguised as a Swedish liner, the SS *Ancona*.

HMS *BELFAST* CRIPPLED BY A MINE

The Germans had a swift revenge for HMS *Belfast*'s early success in capturing the *Cap Norte* when, just before 11.00am on 21 November 1939, when leaving the Firth of Forth, she was blown up by a magnetic mine; the damage was so serious that she lay in Devonport Dockyard for 28 months while repairs were made.

Below **The German liner *Cap Norte* of the Hamburg Sud-American line, captured by HMS *Belfast* on 9 October 1939.**
IWM Neg. No. HU 10272

Bottom **A Royal Marines crew asleep in a turret in HMS *Sheffield,* in 1941. They would have been instantly available if the enemy was detected.**
IWM Neg. No. A 6879

WAR AT SEA 1939–1942

While HMS *Belfast* was undergoing repairs at Devonport, the war at sea continued with increasing fury. The task of the Royal Navy was to ensure that Britain retained control of the seas so that troops could be transported to prosecute the various overseas campaigns in France, Norway and Africa, and also to ensure that the convoys of merchant ships carrying vital food and war materials were safely escorted to the United Kingdom.

The Axis powers attempted to starve Britain into surrender by means of a campaign against merchant shipping using surface raiders and U-boats. The surface raiders inflicted some losses but were dealt with fairly speedily, *Graf Spee* scuttled ignominiously in the River Plate in December 1939 and *Bismarck* battered to a hulk by the guns of the Home Fleet in May 1941. However, the U-boats were a potent menace from the first day of the war until the last. The campaign against the U-boats now known as the Battle of the Atlantic, was the longest of the war and was fought in all weathers in the cruel waters of the North Atlantic.

America's entry into the war proved a decisive factor and, although the U-boats were never defeated, the crushing superiority in numbers and technology possessed by the Allies finally brought the campaign to an end. It was the Allied victory in the Battle of the Atlantic which decided the survival of Great Britain, the freedom of Europe and ultimate victory over the Nazis.

As the war spread first to the Mediterranean and then to the Far East, so the Navy's tasks increased. Ships and resources were overstretched and it was only through the endurance, gallantry and self-sacrifice of the sailors that the Navy held the initiative.

> *'The decisive point in warfare against England lies in attacking her merchant shipping in the Atlantic.'*
> Admiral Doenitz, 1939

HMS *BELFAST* RECOMMISSIONED

HMS *Belfast* recommissioned at Devonport on 3 November 1942 under the command of Captain Frederick Parham and rejoined the Home Fleet as the flagship of the 10th Cruiser Squadron, wearing the flag of Rear Admiral R L Burnett.

Below right **Merchant ships loading tanks for Russia in a British port, 17 October 1941. By the Moscow Protocol of 1 October 1941 the Allies undertook to deliver large quantities of weapons and supplies to the Russians.** IWM Neg. No. H 14785

Bottom **The merchant seamen showed true heroism during their long sea passages in convoys, during which half or more of the ships could be sunk before safety was reached. During the Second World War the British merchant navy lost over 30,000 men and 5,150 Allied merchant ships were sunk as a result of enemy action. The picture shows the ammunition ship *Mary Luckenback* exploding during an air attack on 14 September 1942.** IWM Neg. No. A 12271

HMS *Belfast's* first task after recommissioning was to provide cover for ships of Convoy JW53 which sailed with supplies for Russia on 15 February 1943. This convoy encountered hurricane force gales which scattered the ships and caused severe damage to navy warships and merchant vessels. Most of 1943 was spent in the cold Arctic waters where HMS *Belfast* was employed on patrol, convoy duties and offensive sweeps.

BATTLE OF THE NORTH CAPE, 26 DECEMBER 1943

Between the beginning of November and the middle of December 1943, three eastbound convoys for Russia (JW54A, JW54B and JW55A) and two westbound convoys (RA54A and RA54B) all reached their destinations

without loss thanks to aggressive tactics by HMS *Belfast* and other Allied escorts. However, the Admiralty knew that the German battlecruiser *Scharnhorst* was at Altenfiord in Norway and that it was only a matter of time before she left harbour to attack a convoy.

Convoy JW55B, comprising 19 ships, left Loch Ewe in Scotland for Russia on 20 December 1943. Convoy RA55A consisting of unladen merchant ships left Murmansk on 23 December to return to the United Kingdom. The Admiralty in London took all possible measures to defend the convoys against attack by German ships, and Vice-Admiral Robert Burnett in HMS *Belfast,* which together with HMS *Norfolk* and HMS *Sheffield* formed Force 1, was ready for action from the start. Distant cover was provided by Force 2 under Admiral Bruce Fraser with the battleship HMS *Duke of York,* the cruiser HMS *Jamaica* and a squadron of destroyers, including the Norwegian *Stord.*

The *Scharnhorst,* flying the flag of Rear Admiral Eric Bey, and five large 'Z' class destroyers left Altenfiord on Christmas Day 1943 with the mission to attack and destroy

Left **King George VI on board HMS *Belfast* when visiting the Home Fleet, 15 August 1943.**
IWM Neg. No. A 18689

Bottom left **The sailor – the greatest single factor in fighting a war at sea. It was upon the bravery and determination of ordinary men and women that the outcome of the war depended. The picture shows an Able Seaman in HMS *Belfast* during the period of Russian convoys, in November 1943.**
IWM Neg. No. A 20689

Below **HMS *Holmes* attacks a suspected U-boat, June 1944. German U-boats sank 2,828 Allied merchant ships during the Second World War, causing acute shortages of food and supplies of all kinds. Seven hundred and eighty-five German U-boats were destroyed by Allied forces.**
IWM Neg. No. A 23959

Right The ice-encrusted 6-inch guns of HMS *Belfast's* 'A' and 'B' Turrets are trained ready for action on either beam during convoy duties in northern waters in November 1943.
IWM Neg. No. A 20687

Below right HMS *Belfast* in a gale, 1943. The appalling winter weather was a potent enemy which added to the hardships of the crews in the Arctic convoys.
IWM Neg. No. HU 9144

Below The German battlecruiser *Scharnhorst*. Launched in 1936 and completed in 1939, she displaced 32,000 tons and had a speed of 31.5 knots. With her sister ship the *Gneisenau* she sank the British aircraft carrier HMS *Glorious* off Norway in June 1940. During most of 1941 she remained at Brest, where she was bombed at intervals by the RAF. She escaped to Germany via the English Channel in February 1942 but was sunk at the Battle of North Cape on 26 December 1943. IWM Neg. No. HU 1042

the merchant ships in the convoy. The *Scharnhorst* attacked the cruisers early on 26 December but was driven off after sustaining damage from HMS *Norfolk*. The five German destroyers lost touch with the *Scharnhorst* and played no effective part in the ensuing action. The *Scharnhorst* returned for a second attack at 12.20pm but was again driven off by the cruisers, and Rear Admiral Bey decided to return to the safety of Altenfiord.

As the *Scharnhorst* retreated at high speed the cruisers of Force 1 and the ships of Force 2 gave chase and a salvo from the

> ### 'Sink her with torpedoes.'
>
> Signal C in C Home Fleet
> to HMS *Belfast*
> 26 December 1943, at 7.20pm

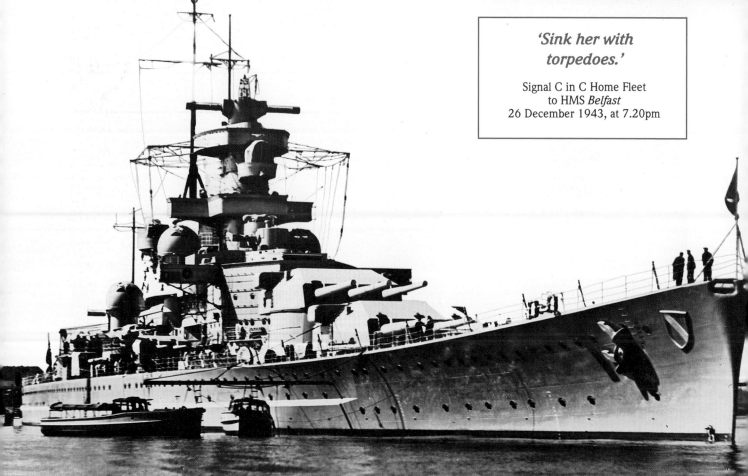

battleship HMS *Duke of York* hit the *Scharnhorst,* reducing her speed. The Allied ships closed in and, as the destruction of the *Scharnhorst* appeared inevitable, Admiral Bey sent a final signal to Berlin – 'We shall fight to the last shell.' The *Scharnhorst* fought bravely but was overwhelmed by the Allied ships and after a fierce action she rolled over and sank. Only thirty-six of her complement of 1,968 men were saved.

OPERATIONS JANUARY – APRIL 1944

With the sinking of the *Scharnhorst,* and the immobilisation of the German battleship *Tirpitz* in a daring attack by British midget submarines, the situation in the Northern Atlantic had been transformed, for the main German surface threat was now eliminated. However, in March intelligence reported that the *Tirpitz* had repaired the damage caused by the midget submarines and was preparing for sea again.

Admiral Fraser planned for two strike forces to carry out an air attack on the *Tirpitz,* with two fleet carriers, HMS *Victorious* and HMS *Furious*, each carrying a strike wing of twenty-one Barracuda bombers. HMS *Belfast* formed part of the escort of this powerful strike force (code-named Operation 'Tungsten'), which carried out a successful raid, hitting the *Tirpitz* with fourteen bombs – putting her out of action until she was finally sunk by bombers of the RAF.

Left **Battle damage in HMS *Norfolk* after the Battle of North Cape. During the action against the *Scharnhorst* on 26 December 1943, the only ship to sustain serious damage on the Allied side was HMS *Norfolk*, which was hit by one salvo and suffered seven killed and five seriously wounded. The picture shows the passage of an 11-inch shell across her deck.** IWM Neg. No. FL 5870

Below **Barracuda aircraft attack the *Tirpitz*, 3 April 1944.** IWM Neg. No. A 22631

D-DAY, 6 JUNE 1944

The plan for the invasion of Europe (code-named Operation 'Overlord') provided for an attack on a fifty-mile stretch of the Normandy coast by a force of five divisions, with additional landings aimed at the port of Cherbourg.

The naval part of the invasion plan, Operation 'Neptune', aimed 'to secure lodgement on the continent from which further offensive operations can be developed' and the naval forces were allocated for escort duties, mine-sweeping, gunfire support to the army, and the defence of the hundreds of vessels carrying food, water, stores, ammunition and reinforcement troops.

The actual assault was to be carried out by two large amphibious forces called the Eastern and Western Naval Task Forces. HMS *Belfast* was part of the Eastern force, which was mainly British, and was commanded by Rear Admiral Sir Philip Vian who had the task

of landing three divisions of the British Second Army in three sectors called Sword, Juno and Gold.

The warships allocated to Operation Neptune totalled 1,213 vessels, ranging from large battleships and monitors down to midget submarines. HMS *Belfast* formed part of the massive bombardment force which gathered in Belfast Lough and was matched by ships assembled in the Clyde.

At 5.30am on 6 June 1944 HMS *Belfast,* commanded by Captain F R Parham DSO RN, fired the first shells of the invasion at the German battery at Ver sur Mer. At 7.30am the assault forces, launched from further out at sea, passed HMS *Belfast* and stormed the beaches. The Seventh Battalion of the Green Howards overran the 10-cm battery, where the German gunners were hiding in their bunkers, their guns having been destroyed by HMS *Belfast*'s shells.

> **'Pro Tanto Quid Retribuamus.'**
>
> **'For so much how shall we repay?'**
>
> The Motto of HMS *Belfast* and of the City of Belfast

Below right **HMS *Belfast*'s 4-inch guns in action at night off the Normandy beach-head, 27 June 1944.** IWM Neg. No. A 24325

Below **A sailor in festive mood preparing for Christmas at sea in HMS *Turquoise,* an escort trawler, in 1944.**
IWM Neg. No. A 21073

HMS *Belfast* remained in the Channel area until 10 July, carrying out bombardment of enemy targets ashore and helping to protect the other ships in the Task Force against surface attack. Her 6-inch guns had fired in anger for the last time during the war in Europe. She now prepared to sail to the Far East, ready to help in the fight against Japan.

HMS *BELFAST* IN THE FAR EAST, 1945–1947

The atomic bombs had exploded over Hiroshima and Nagasaki and the Japanese had surrendered before HMS *Belfast* arrived at Sydney but there was much work to be done rescuing the emaciated survivors of the Japanese prison camps. HMS *Belfast* was engaged in ferrying the sick and dying between Shanghai and Hong Kong. To the freed British prisoners, the sight of the warships proudly flying the White Ensign would remain an enduring memory.

The missions of mercy were completed by January 1946 but HMS *Belfast* remained in the Far East performing a peace-keeping role during a period of general unrest in South East Asia and the East Indies. She eventually returned to Portsmouth on 15 October 1947, where she paid off into reserve.

THE KOREAN WAR, 1950–1952

HMS *Belfast* remained at Portsmouth for a year, during which time she was armed with four more Bofors guns. She recommissioned on 22 September 1948 under Captain E K Le Mesurier and visited the city where she had been built to receive a gift from the people of Belfast – the magnificent silver bell which now hangs proudly on her Quarterdeck. On 23 October 1948 she sailed again for the Far East, reaching Hong Kong at the end of December to become the flagship of the 5th Cruiser Squadron commanded by Rear Admiral A C G Madden.

The Communist insurgency in Malaya had already begun and Mao Tse Tung's forces were poised to overthrow the Nationalist regime in China. For the next 18 months, as tension mounted, HMS *Belfast* helped safeguard British interests in this troubled area of

Left **These children have just completed a ride in a swinging crate suspended from HMS *Belfast*'s crane, at a party for young internees at Shanghai in September 1945.** IWM Neg. No. A 30854

Below **'A' and 'B' Turrets firing a salvo at shore targets off Korea in 1951. During the Korean War HMS *Belfast* fired so many salvoes that she wore out her 6-inch guns and had to return to Singapore to have 12 replacement barrels fitted.** IWM Neg. No. A 32031

the world. The Korean War started when the Communist forces of North Korea crossed the 38th Parallel on 25 June 1950 to invade South Korea. Great Britain, America and other United Nations forces were quickly involved and HMS *Belfast* led British and Commonwealth ships into action on 6 July 1950, bombarding shore targets to support the hard-pressed troops on land.

In October 1950 HMS *Belfast* was ordered to return home to recommission. The ship stayed in Chatham for 17 days and sailed again for the Far East with a full war complement embarked. On arrival off Korea in February 1951 the bitter fighting was still in progress, with the Chinese forces being driven back slowly to the 38th Parallel. As the opposing armies fought up and down the Korean peninsula so United Nations ships moved with them, bombarding, blockading, mine-sweeping and evacuating.

HMS *Belfast*'s operations off Korea continued throughout 1951 and 1952 with the by now familiar operations of bombardment, harassment and interdiction of enemy forces. Although she had caused immense havoc to the Communists, it was not until 29 July 1952 that the ship was hit by return fire when a 76 mm shell struck, killing one Chinese laundryman and injuring four others.

HMS *Belfast* leaving Singapore on 26 March 1962 at the end of her final foreign service commission. She is flying a Rear Admiral's flag at the foremast.
IWM Neg. No. HU 4646

> ‘That straight-shooting ship!’
>
> ascribed to American Admiral describing HMS *Belfast*

Peace in Korea The Korean War ended on 26 September 1952. After over two years of bitter fighting, both sides were back to where they started. HMS *Belfast* returned to the UK and, after three years in reserve, was modernised in Devonport for the second time in her life. She recommissioned on 12 May 1959 ready to meet the challenges of the modern Navy.

EAST OF SUEZ AGAIN, 1959–1962

HMS *Belfast* sailed for the Far East and spent the years 1959–1962 performing the usual duties of HM ships abroad in peacetime – carrying out exercises and generally ‘showing the flag’.

One notable event occurred in December 1961 when HMS *Belfast* entered Dar-es-Salaam to take part in the granting of independence to Tanganyika. She had the

honour of providing the guard for the final hauling down of the Union Flag and the first hoisting of the Tanganyikan flag. Thousands thronged the foreshore as HMS *Belfast* steamed out of Dar-es-Salaam harbour.

FINAL COMMISSION 1963

HMS *Belfast* returned to the UK and made a final visit to the City of Belfast. Following one last exercise in the Mediterranean she finally paid off in Devonport on 24 August 1963 and her Admiral's flag was hauled down for the last time. She had earned her rest, having steamed nearly half a million miles during her operational life.

> *'The Royal Navy of England hath ever been its greatest defence and ornament; its ancient and natural strength, the floating bulwark of the island.'*
>
> Sir William Blackston
> *Commentaries,* 1765–1769

HMS *BELFAST* – MUSEUM SHIP

In the normal course of events, her next destination would very probably have been the scrapyard. However, behind the scenes, a determined group of men led by her former captain, now Rear Admiral, Sir Morgan Morgan-Giles DSO OBE GM, decided to save her and she was brought to London and opened to the public on 21 October 1971 – Trafalgar Day.

HMS *Belfast* is now part of the Imperial War Museum and is the first ship to be preserved for the nation since Nelson's *Victory*.

With her top-mast just clearing the upper-works of Tower Bridge, HMS *Belfast* arrives in the Pool of London on 14 October 1971 – her final resting place after years of active service for her country.
IWM Neg. No. MH 15063

GENERAL INFORMATION

OPENING HOURS AND ADMISSION

OPEN SEVEN DAYS A WEEK THROUGHOUT THE YEAR EXCEPT 24, 25, 26 DECEMBER

Summer (1 March – 31 October)
Open 10.00 am – 6.00 pm
(last admission 5.15 pm)

Winter (1 November – 28 February)
Open 10.00 pm – 5.00 pm
(last admission 4.15 pm)

An admission fee is charged. Reductions are available for children (5–16 years), students, disabled persons, senior citizens and registered unemployed. Additional discounts are available for families (two adults and two or more children) and for groups (ten or more).

REFRESHMENTS The Walrus Café in Zone 3 serves a variety of cooked meals, hot and cold drinks, snacks, sandwiches and confectionery. The café is open seven days a week from 10.30 am.

GIFT SHOP Situated on the riverside, the shop stocks a full range of souvenirs and gifts, including postcards, books, posters and prints, model kits and videos. No admission ticket is required for entry to the shop. For those unable to visit the shop a mail order service is available, including a full colour mail order catalogue. Telephone 0171–407 6434 ext. 34 for further details.

FERRY A ferry service operates between HMS *Belfast*'s Quarterdeck and Tower Pier on the north bank of the Thames. The service runs at 15-minute intervals from 11.00 am to closing time every day during its summer season (1 April – 30 September); at weekends and half-term only during October; in the week immediately after Christmas and in half-term week in February. A special service is provided over Easter holiday periods in March.

TOILETS Toilets are situated close to the Quarterdeck (where visitors come on board) in Zone 1, and towards the bow of the ship in Zone 3.

ACCESS FOR THE DISABLED The Imperial War Museum is a member of the Museums and Galleries Disability Association. Every effort is being made to make HMS *Belfast* as accessible to disabled visitors as possible. A wheelchair lift provides access to the ship, with entry to the upper deck via special ramps. A disabled toilet has been installed close to the main entrance. For details of these and other services for the disabled please contact the Education Officer on 0171–407 6434 ext. 20.

MEETING POINT The Quarterdeck is the suggested meeting point for all visitors, either boarding or leaving the ship. A member of staff is on duty here at all times and a broadcast system is available, if necessary, to pipe an emergency message to visitors.

FRIENDS OF THE IMPERIAL WAR MUSEUM HMS *Belfast* is a branch of the Imperial War Museum. Friends of the Imperial War Museum are granted the privilege of free admission to all its branches. Benefits also include private viewings of new exhibitions, lectures and film shows, a regular newsletter, and discounts in the Museum's shops. The Friends of the Imperial War Museum is a Registered Charity, No. 294360. For further details, please contact the Friends of the Imperial War Museum, Imperial War Museum, Lambeth Road, London SE1 6HZ, or telephone 0171–416 5255.

DONATIONS It costs almost £1,000 a day to preserve and maintain this historic warship. Donations are always most welcome and should be addressed to the Director, HMS *Belfast*, Morgans Lane, Tooley Street, London SE1 2JH, or placed in the large black and white mine on the Quarterdeck.

Top **HMS *Belfast*'s shop.**

Right **Tables set for a private reception aboard HMS *Belfast*.**

Photo: Hartley, Nock, Walker

CORPORATE HOSPITALITY Ring and Brymer, with over 300 years' experience, is the City of London's foremost specialist in catering for prestige events. The Admiral's Quarters, Wardroom and Anteroom, the Ship's Company Dining Hall and the Gunroom banqueting suites can be hired for receptions, lunches, dinners and conferences, and a full catering service is available. For full details, please contact the Catering Manager on board (telephone 0171–403 6246).

EDUCATIONAL FACILITIES

From the crowded conditions of the hammock-slung messdecks to the re-creation of a surface battle in the Operations Room, a visit to HMS *Belfast* provides a unique opportunity for children of all ages. By exploring all seven decks of this huge and complex warship they will discover naval history in the twentieth century for themselves.

Illustrated talks, films and activity sessions are available to all pre-booked school groups, offering scope for a wide framework of curricular studies from Key Stage 1 onwards. As an additional guide around the ship, quiz trails are available with project sheets for younger children to complete at school or at home. Full details, plus a booking form, can be found in the Teachers' Information Pack, available on request. Preliminary visits by teachers are welcome and are free if booked in advance.

Children with learning difficulties are especially welcome, and there are plenty of hands-on areas to explore in addition to the facilities available in the classroom. Pupils may be given an opportunity to handle such items as a 6-inch shell, try on naval uniforms or be strapped into a special ship's stretcher. Many areas on board employ exciting sound and light effects to help bring the ship to life. All talks are flexible in content and can be adapted to suit the requirements of each group.

Please note that educational facilities are not available at weekends.

A packed lunch area seating up to 25 is available, with additional space on the upper deck in fine weather. **The packed lunch area is also popular as a free venue for birthday parties on board, which include a free birthday pack.** Please contact the Education Officer for further details.

A selection of primary resource material is available by mail order from the Imperial War Museum, including videos, document sets, facsimile posters and cassettes. Please contact the Sales Officer, Marketing and Trading, at the Imperial War Museum, Lambeth Road, London SE1 6HZ, or telephone 0171–416 5396 for a catalogue.

The education staff are always seeking to improve their services to schools and any comments or suggestions by teachers are most welcome.

For further information and booking forms, please contact the Education Officer on 0171–407 6434.

Above **A lively group of middle school children learning about life between decks in HMS *Belfast*'s well-equipped Educational Facilities Suite.**
IWM Neg. No. 96/75/6

Published by the Imperial War Museum,
Lambeth Road, London SE1 6HZ.

Revised edition © The Trustees of the Imperial War Museum 1997
ISBN 1 870423 17 8

Designed by Peter Dolton.
Design and production in association with
Book Production Consultants PLC, 25–27 High Street, Chesterton, Cambridge CB4 1ND.
Colour photography by Reeve Photography, Cambridge, Paul Cordwell and Imperial War Museum.
Cover photograph by Glyn Williams.
Film origination by J Film Process Limited.
Printed and bound in England by George Over Limited, Rugby.

Part of your family's history

Imperial War Museum
Lambeth Road
London SE1 6HZ

Tel: 0171-416 5000

The nerve centre of Britain's war effort

Cabinet War Rooms
Clive Steps
King Charles Street
London SW1A 2AQ

Tel: 0171-930 6961

More than a museum

Duxford Airfield
Duxford
Cambridge CB2 4QR

Tel: Cambridge
01223-833963